Say Hello to CACTUS FLATS

A FoxTrot Collection
by Bill Amend

Andrews and McMeel
A Universal Press Syndicate
Kansas City

FoxTrot is distributed internationally by Universal Press Syndicate.

Say Hello to Cactus Flats copyright © 1993 by Bill Amend. All rights reserved. Printed in the United States of America. No part of this book may be used or reproduced in any manner whatsoever without written permission except in the case of reprints in the context of reviews. For information write Andrews and McMeel, a Universal Press Syndicate Company, 4900 Main Street, Kansas City, Missouri 64112.

ISBN: 0-8362-1720-9

Library of Congress Catalog Card Number: 93-71039

Printed on recycled paper.

──── ATTENTION: SCHOOLS AND BUSINESSES ────

Andrews and McMeel books are available at quantity discounts for bulk purchase for educational, business, or sales promotional use. For information, please write to Special Sales Department, Andrews and McMeel, 4900 Main Street, Kansas City, Missouri 64112.

HI! I'M REGIS! AND HI! I'M KATHIE LEE!

OUR GUESTS TODAY INCLUDE EMILIO ESTEVEZ, WHO'S PROMOTING HIS NEW MOVIE... JACKIE COLLINS, WHO'S PROMOTING HER NEW BOOK... AND DANA CARVEY, WHO'S PROMOTING HIS NEW BOB KERREY IMPRESSION.

BUT FIRST, LET'S PROMOTE OURSELVES. GOOD IDEA. SO HOW'R CODY AND FRANK?

I NEED MORE ASPIRIN, MOM. CUTE AS EVER. MIND IF I SING? ONLY IF I CAN'T JOIN IN...

I GET TO STAY HOME FROM SCHOOL...

I GET TO LIE IN BED AND WATCH SOAPS ALL DAY...

HACK COUGH COUGH HACK SNIFFLE COUGH HACK COUGH GAG COUGH SNIFFLE COUGH COUGH GUNK ICK COUGH WHEEZ HACK COUGH COUGH COUGH COUGH HACK UGGH.

I KNEW THERE HAD TO BE A CATCH. SWEETIE, YOU LOOK AWFUL.

COUGH.

COUGH COUGH.

COUGH COUGH COUGH.

I APPRECIATE YOUR CONCERN, BUT—... CONCERN, NOTHING— I'VE GOT A MATH TEST TOMORROW. TIME'S UP. MY TURN.

6

by Bill Amend

ON YOUR MARK... GET SET...

GET SET... GET SET... GET SET...

WHAT ARE YOU DOING?

GETTING READY FOR THE NEW SPRINGSTEEN ALBUMS.

THE NEWSPAPER SAID THEY'D BE OUT ANY DAY NOW, SO I NEED TO BE PREPARED TO DASH OFF TO THE STORE ON A MOMENT'S NOTICE.

I WAS SEVENTEENTH IN LINE FOR "TUNNEL OF LOVE," BUT THAT WAS BEFORE I COULD DRIVE.

MAN, I MUST'VE BLASTED THAT ALBUM 3,000 TIMES THE FIRST DAY ALONE. I NEARLY BLEW MY SPEAKERS.

AMEND

ANYWAY, THAT'S WHAT I'M DOING.

I, UM, WAS ASKING THEM...

MY STEREO!

YOU'LL GET IT BACK. SOMEDAY.

PAIGE, WATCH THE WIRES.

SO THERE'S WHERE MY MADONNA TAPE WENT!

IT WAS AWFUL. FIRST PAIGE CAME DOWN WITH THE FLU, THEN PETER, THEN JASON.

I FELT LIKE I WAS RUNNING A SICK WARD ALL WEEKEND.

I COULDN'T IMAGINE A MORE MISERABLE SCENARIO.

THEN CAME MONDAY.

CAN YOU OPEN THE ASPIRIN FOR ME?

I'M DYING, ANDY. I'M GIVING UP THE GHOST.

EVERY CELL IN MY BEING IS CRYING OUT IN ANGUISH.

IT WAS A GOOD LIFE WHILE IT LASTED, BUT THIS IS IT. HELLO, GRIM REAPER.

HONESTLY. THIS MEDICINE CAN'T TASTE **THAT** BAD.

I... I SEE ELVIS...

COULD YOU HEAT UP SOME CHICKEN SOUP FOR ME?

ROGER, I'M REALLY BUSY RIGHT NOW. YOU'LL JUST HAVE TO FEND FOR YOURSELF.

BUT I'M SICK.

GOOD GRIEF— WE'RE NOT TALKING BRAIN SURGERY. ALL YOU HAVE TO DO IS OPEN A STUPID CAN AND DUMP IT INTO A POT.

NOW WHAT?

NOW WE TALK BRAIN SURGERY.

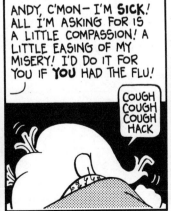

I TELL YOU, THE WARRIORS LOOK MORE AND MORE LIKE THE TEAM TO BEAT.

OF COURSE, YOU CAN'T DISCOUNT PORTLAND. THEY'RE MOST LIKELY STILL THE TEAM TO BEAT.

AND THE BULLS, WELL, THEY'RE JUST ON FIRE. DEFINITELY THE TEAM TO BEAT.

BUT THE CELTICS LOOK OK. COULD BE THE REAL TEAM TO BEAT.

CAN'T FORGET THE KNICKS. AT HOME THEY'RE PROBABLY STILL THE TEAM TO BEAT.

OOO—THE JAZZ. NOW **THERE'S** THE TEAM TO BEAT.

ASK ME WHOM **I'D** LIKE TO BEAT...

HERE?

NOW?

THANK YOU.

GREETINGS, EVIL VILLAIN.

AND WELCOME TO TONIGHT'S INSTALLMENT OF "THE YOUNG INDIANA JONES CHRONICLES." I'M 10-YEAR-OLD INDY, THIS EPISODE'S FEATURED ADVENTURER.

AMEND

AÂAÂAAA!

THE END.

KATHWAP!

MOTH-ERRR!....

AND NOW FOR A PREVIEW OF NEXT WEEK'S SHOW...

GREETINGS, EVIL VILLAIN.

HOW'S YOUR DINNER, INDY-10?

YUMMY. HOW'S YOURS, INDY-16?

GOOD. IT REMINDS ME OF THE CUISINE OF THE TRIBES-MEN OF NEW GUINEA. THEY, OF COURSE, USE A HEAVIER SAUCE.

YOU'RE FORGETTING I HAVEN'T BEEN THERE YET.

AMEND

AH, YES. IT'LL BE THE SPRING OF 1914. YOU'LL HAVE FUN. OH, BY THE WAY, THEY'LL WANT YOUR HEAD.

SEEMS EVERY-ONE DOES.

I CAN ONLY SPEAK FOR ME, BUT—...

I LEARNED A NEW LANGUAGE TODAY...

GUYS, THIS "YOUNG INDIANA JONES" STUFF HAS GOT TO STOP.

IF YOU DID THIS FOR FIVE MINUTES, IT MIGHT BE FUNNY. IF YOU DID IT FOR 10 MINUTES IT MIGHT BE FUNNY. BUT YOU'VE BEEN PLAYING THIS LITTLE GAME ALL WEEK!

SO?

SO?! YOUR SISTER'S ON THE VERGE OF A BREAKDOWN!

SOUNDS FUNNY TO ME.

THE HATS. NOW.

GOOD ONE, INDY-10.

IF YOU FLEW US TO CAIRO LIKE WE ASKED...

by Bill Amend

FoxTrot

SKREET
SKREET
SKREET

LAY ON,
MACFOX...

From the very first act, Shakespeare's <u>Macbeth</u> presents challenges and questions to the reader on a number of levels.

Do the unflattering portrayals of women -- notably the witches and Lady Macbeth -- reveal a misogynistic leaning on the part of the author?

What is the significance of the "moving" forest? Is Shakespeare using this imagery to symbolize man's desire to bend and control the natural order?

And what of Lady Macbeth's forever-bloodied hands? Is this meant as a doctrinal stance on the redemptability of the mortally sinful?

These are all legitimate issues. But I will devote this essay to the exploration of a different question. One that looms throughout the work.

"WHAT'S WITH ALL THE 'PRITHEES'?"!

MOM, C'MON, JUST CHECK THE SPELLING.

AMEND

YAWN.

DAAAAAAAAD!

I GUESS HE GOT MY HINT.

YOU KNOW, WE **DO** HAVE POST-IT NOTES.

AMEND

AH, SPRING.

THE SWEET SONG OF BIRDS CHIRPING... THE SWEET SMELL OF FLOWERS BLOOMING... THE SWEET SOUND OF LAWN MOWERS MOWING...

AMEND

I SAID, THE SWEET SOUND OF—...

WHY CAN'T **JASON** DO THIS?!

PETER, THINK OF THIS AS CHARACTER-BUILDING.

THINK OF THIS AS EXERCISE.

AMEND

THINK OF THIS AS FUN.

FUN?!

WELL, HECK, IF YOU BOUGHT THE FIRST TWO...

DON'T YOU HAVE TO GO PLAY GOLF OR SOMETHING?

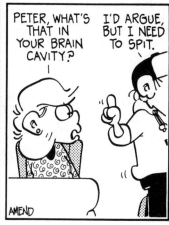

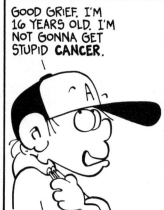

MOM, C'MON, I'M 16. I THINK I'M OLD ENOUGH TO HANDLE AN OCCASIONAL DIP. AGE HAS NOTHING TO DO WITH IT.

PETER, NICOTINE'S ONE OF THE MOST ADDICTIVE DRUGS THERE IS! AS I SEE IT, YOU'VE GOT THREE OPTIONS: YOU CAN QUIT NOW, WHILE IT'S EASY; QUIT LATER, WHEN IT'S NEAR IMPOSSIBLE; OR QUIT BY DEFAULT WHEN THEY REMOVE YOUR CANCEROUS JAW!

AMEND

YOU KNOW, WHERE'S THE FUN IN EASY? WHERE'S THE FUN IN CHEWING THAT STUFF?

MOM, STOP WORRYING! I CAN QUIT WHENEVER I WANT!

I'VE ONLY BEEN CHEWING THE STUFF FOR THREE WEEKS —YOU DON'T TURN INTO AN ADDICT OVERNIGHT!

AMEND

I COULD STOP DIPPING ALTOGETHER RIGHT THIS INSTANT AND IT WOULDN'T AFFECT ME ONE IOTA! THEN DO. NOW.

I SORTA MEANT THIS INSTANT, LIKE, TOMORROW. NOW.

YOU'VE QUIT CHEWING TOBACCO AND YOU'RE BETTER OFF FOR HAVING DONE SO.

YOU'VE QUIT CHEWING TOBACCO AND YOU'RE BETTER OFF FOR HAVING DONE SO.

YOU'VE QUIT—... BZZZ-ZZZZ!

THIS MAY BE HARDER THAN I THOUGHT. RISE AND SHINE, ROCKERS! LET'S CHECK THE FORECAST...

AMEND

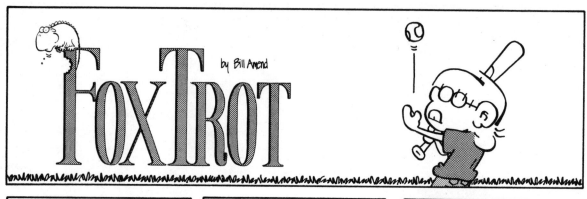

by Bill Amend

FoxTrot

BONK!

STEEE-RIKE ONE.

STEEE-RIKE TWO.

AND WE GO TO THE BOTTOM OF THE 138TH, STILL TIED AT ZERO.

MY DAD SAYS THESE ARE THE BEST KINDA GAMES.

GREETINGS, UGLY EARTHLING. I AM IGUANOMAN.

NOT **THIS** AGAIN!

YES, INDEED. I HAVE RE- TURNED TO YOUR PLANET TO FURTHER EVALUATE YOUR SPECIES.

JASON, **PLEASE**...

MY ORDERS ARE TO STUDY AND OBSERVE YOU, PAIGE FOX, IN PARTICULAR.

MOTH- ERRR!

AMEND

I MUST CONFESS I HAD A SIMILAR REACTION.

TELL ME, DO THEY EVEN **HAVE** A COUNSELOR AT YOUR SCHOOL?

WILL YOU QUIT FOLLOWING ME **AROUND**?!

I TOLD YOU, I WAS SENT HERE TO OBSERVE YOU.

THE IGUANOPEOPLE OF MY PLANET WANT TO KNOW EVERYTHING ABOUT YOU, PAIGE FOX. WHAT YOU EAT... WHAT YOU DRINK...

WHY YOUR FELLOW HUMANS HAVEN'T BANISHED YOU TO SOME GOD-FORSAKEN DESERT ISLAND...

DON'T THINK I WOULDN'T LEAP AT THE CHANCE.

THAT FUNGUS ON YOUR HEAD—IS THAT WHAT YOU CALL "HAIR"?

AMEND

IGUANOMAN'S LOG, STARDATE 9540.263π: SUBJECT IS SHOWING ES- CALATING SIGNS OF ANNOY- ANCE.

PROBABLE CAUSE: THE PROXIMITY OF MY SUPERIOR INTELLECT IS CHALLENGING HER SELF- WORTH.

I MUST CONCLUDE THAT CONTINUED OBSERVATION WILL NO DOUBT LEAD TO AN UGLY CONFRONTATION. ONE OF DEVASTATING MAGNITUDE.

SO NATURALLY YOU'RE NOT GOING TO STOP.

SUBJECT IS SHOWING SIGNS OF TELEPATHY...

SUBJECT IS SHAKING UP HER COKE CAN...

AMEND

JASON, WILL YOU LEAVE ME **ALONE**?!

WHY DO YOU INSIST ON CALLING ME "JASON"?

BECAUSE THAT'S YOUR NAME, YOU LITTLE NERD-BAG!

I BELIEVE WE'VE GONE OVER THIS BEFORE. MY NAME IS IGUANOMAN.

AAAA! THIS JASON FELLOW MUST BE RATHER BRILLIANT AND GOOD-LOOKING FOR YOU TO CONTINUALLY GET US MIXED UP LIKE THIS.

AMEND

YOU'RE CALLING **ME** MIXED UP?!

EXCUSE ME WHILE I PREPARE A RESPONSE.

AS MUCH AS I HATE TO JOIN IN HERE..

BUT MADAM, I WAS ONLY **OBSERVING** PAIGE. SURELY THAT'S NOT A CRIME.

YOU WERE DRIVING HER NUTS. NOW OFF TO YOUR ROOM.

THAT MAY BE RATHER DIFFI-CULT, SEEING AS MY "ROOM" IS ON A PLANET 3.27 TRILLION LIGHT-YEARS AWAY.

THEN YOU'D BETTER START WALKING.

ONE DOESN'T "WALK" 3.27 TRILLION LIGHT-YEARS, ONE "WARPS."

NOW!

UM, ALLOW ME TO DEMONSTRATE.

I ASSUME THEY HAVE **HOMEWORK** ON YOUR PLANET...

BUT MADAM, I SIMPLY SEEK SUSTENANCE.

I'M SORRY, BUT IGUANOMAN IS NOT WELCOME AT THE DINNER TABLE.

TYPICAL HUMAN SNOBBERY.

IF YOU WANT TO COME BACK AS JASON, YOU CAN JOIN US.

HI, MADAM— I MEAN, "MOM"...

YOU REALLY SAVOR THIS, DON'T YOU?

AMEND

by Bill Amend

DRIBBLE DRIBBLE
DRIBBLE DRIBBLE
DRIBBLE

CRUNCH

STUPID SNAILS...

MULLIN MOVES THE BALL UPCOURT...

HE PASSES TO HARDAWAY, WHO DOES HIS KILLER CROSSOVER...

A NO-LOOK PASS TO MARCIULIONIS...HE DRIVES INTO THE PAINT...

HE KICKS IT OUT TO HILL... FIVE SECONDS ON THE SHOT CLOCK...

HILL LOFTS AN ALLEY-OOP TO OWENS, WHO TAKES IT IN FOR THE—...

SLAM!

THE CROWD ERUPTS WITH APPLAUSE.

DON NELSON CALLS A 20-HOUR TIMEOUT...

AMEND

HAVE YOU SEEN THAT NEW ART GALLERY OVER ON MAIN STREET?

NO. WHY?

MARCUS AND I WANDERED IN THERE TODAY. IT WAS INCREDIBLE.

OH?

I MEAN, TALK ABOUT INSPIRING. TALK ABOUT EYE-OPENING. THE TWO OF US WERE JUST STANDING THERE IN AWE.

OF THE ART?

OF THE PRICES. WHERE'RE MY CRAYONS?

LOOK, LEROY, BEFORE YOU GET **TOO** EXCITED...

I NEVER KNEW ART COULD BE LIKE THIS.

PASS THE RED PAINT.

SO ENRICHING... SO REWARDING... SO... SO...

LUCRATIVE?

HOW'S IT LOOK?

Limited Edition Slug-Man Cartoons!!! $99 97 each! Dealers Welcome

ARE YOU READY TO FEAST YOUR EYES ON THE LATEST OF MY SURE-FIRE PATHS TO FAME AND RICHES?

I DOUBT IT.

PRESENTING "SLUG-MAN SUITABLE FOR FRAMING LIMITED EDITION REPRODUCTIONS."

GOOD LORD.

EACH IS HAND-SIGNED AND NUMBERED BY THE ARTIST (ME) AND WOULD MAKE AN ATTRACTIVE WALL HANGING THAT WOULD COMPLEMENT ANY DECOR. BE SURE TO BUY YOURS TODAY — AT THE LOW PRICE OF ONLY $99.97, THESE BEAUTIES WON'T LAST LONG.

$99.97?! FOR A SLUG-MAN CARTOON?!

AH, I SENSE EXCITEMENT IN YOUR VOICE.

AND PRINTED ON SUCH FINE XEROX STOCK, TOO...

WELL, OF **COURSE** THEY'RE XEROXES. THAT'S THE BEAUTY OF LIMITED EDITIONS.

I ONLY HAVE TO DO ONE DRAWING, LOTS OF PEOPLE GET TO BUY THEM, THE PRICES FLIRT WITH AFFORDABLE, MY PROFIT IS HUMONGOUS AND I STILL GET TO KEEP THE ORIGINAL ART ON **MY** WALL.

IT'S ONE OF THOSE WONDERFUL SITUATIONS WHERE EVERYBODY WINS.

...OR AT LEAST I DO.

YOU KNOW, FOR $100 EACH, YOU'D THINK YOU'D HAVE CLEANED THE GLASS BETTER.

WHAT'S WRONG WITH IT?!

JASON, YOU CAN'T SELL **XEROXES** FOR $100 **EACH!**

THEY'RE NOT **JUST** XEROXES, MOTHER! EACH IS A HANDSIGNED AND NUMBERED LIMITED EDITION SUITABLE FOR FRAMING SLUG-MAN REPRODUCTION! THEY'RE COLLECTOR'S ITEMS!

IF YOU ASK **ME**, AT $99.97 EACH THEY'RE A **STEAL**.

YES, BUT ON WHOSE PART?

HMM. BAD CHOICE OF WORDS.

I'LL BUY ONE FOR A **QUARTER**...

A **QUARTER**?! MOTHER, YOU INSULT ME!

JASON, C'MON— HOW MUCH DO YOU HONESTLY THINK THESE ARE **WORTH**?!

WELL... THE LIMITED EDITION STUFF THEY HAD AT THE ART GALLERY COST LIKE $1,000. SELLING THESE FOR $99.97 SEEMED LIKE A BARGAIN.

AND MAYBE IT **WILL BE** SOMEDAY.

SOMEDAY?

JASON, IT TAKES AN ESTABLISHED ARTIST TO COMMAND THOSE BIG PRICES AND IT TAKES YEARS OF HARD WORK TO BECOME ESTABLISHED. YOU'RE JUST STARTING OUT— GIVE THINGS **TIME.**

I SUPPOSE IT WOULDN'T HURT TO HOARD THEM FOR A **LITTLE** WHILE...

I CAN EVEN GUARANTEE APPRECIATION.

FoxTrot

by Bill Amend

KA THWAP!

ZZZZ

ZZZZ

HAPPY MOTHER'S DAY, MOM.

WHY, THANK YOU, SWEETIE.

AMEND

SO WHAT'D YOU THINK OF THE MATH TEST THIS MORNING?

I THINK I DID OK.

WHAT'D YOU GET FOR THE FIRST QUESTION?

UM... $\frac{1}{2} \sin\theta\cos\theta$.

WHAT'D YOU GET FOR THE SECOND QUESTION?

WHAT'D **YOU** GET FOR THE FIRST QUESTION?

I HAD A DOCTOR'S APPOINTMENT. I'M TAKING THE TEST AT LUNCH.

WHOOPS— DID I SAY ONE **HALF** $\sin\theta\cos\theta$?

PETER, C'MON— I'M TAKING THE TEST IN FIVE MINUTES—WHAT'D YOU GET FOR THE BONUS QUESTION?

STEVE, I DON'T THINK I WANT TO TELL YOU.

PETE, PETE, PETE— IT'S **ME**, YOUR BUDDY, **STEVE**— WHAT'D YOU GET?

I'M NOT SAYING.

YOU DIDN'T GET IT, DID YOU.

YOU DON'T GET IT, **DO** YOU?

PETER, GEEZ— THIS ISN'T **CHEATING**.

SURE SEEMS LIKE IT.

"CHEATING" WOULD BE IF I KNEW THE CORRECT ANSWERS AHEAD OF TIME.

ALL I'M DOING IS ASKING YOU WHAT **YOUR** ANSWERS WERE.

WHAT'S THE DIFFERENCE?

NO OFFENSE, BUT—...

GOOD**BYE**, STEVE.

STUPID STEVE.

WHAT'S WRONG?

HE WANTED ME TO GIVE HIM ALL THE ANSWERS TO THE MATH TEST.

DID YOU?

OF COURSE NOT. BUT NOW I FEEL ALL GUILTY. HE MADE IT SEEM LIKE I WAS SOMEHOW BETRAYING OUR FRIENDSHIP.

MMM.

I WASN'T, WAS I?

NOW **YOU** WANT THE EASY ANSWERS, I SEE...

I CAN'T BELIEVE STEVE PUT ME IN THIS SITUATION.

TELL HIM THAT.

IF I'D GIVEN HIM THE ANSWERS, I'D HAVE COMPROMISED MY INTEGRITY, DONE HIM A DISSERVICE AND SCREWED UP MY AND EVERYONE ELSE'S GRADE.

TELL HIM THAT.

BUT BY **NOT** HELPING HIM CHEAT, I NOW FEEL LIKE I'M SOME SORT OF TRAITOR — AND I **SHOULDN'T**. I MEAN, **HE'S** THE ONE WHO SHOULD FEEL BAD. **HE'S** THE ONE WHO CROSSED THE LINE, NOT **ME**.

TELL HIM THAT.

SO, UM, WHAT SHOULD I DO?

TELL ME SOMETHING...

STEVE.

PETE.

YOU KNOW...

I KNOW...

AND WOMEN SAY MEN NEVER TALK.

CATCH THE GAME LAST NIGHT?

30

FoxTrot by Bill Amend

The Adventures of **Slug-Man** by Jason Fox — Episode 4

...,030,461

When we last left our fearless duo, Slug-Man and Leech-Boy were in the Slug Cave, honing their martial arts skills.

Hiyaa!

Holy broken I-beams!

crack!

Pons

Suddenly, a familiar beacon penetrates the night sky high above stately Slug Manor!!!

To the Slug-mobile, Leech-Boy!

At Jasonopolis police headquarters, Commissioner Jones explains the situation: the vile Paige-o-tron is on the loose.

The vile Paige-o-tron is on the loose.

Uh-oh.

Uh-oh.

Suddenly, Commissioner Jones pulls off his skin to reveal that he is really Paige-o-tron in disguise!!!

It's Paige-o-tron!!!

Ha! Ha! Ha!

Yes, Paige-o-tron, that robotic cauldron of all that is wretched and evil, has once again surfaced to do battle with our heroes!

Give it up, Paige-o-tron!

Never!!

Fortunately for Slug-Man, Paige-o-tron is predictable.

Aaaa! I missed!

zap!

You always do.

Fortunately for Slug-Man, Paige-o-tron is weak.

Get off me, you slug!

That's Slug-Man.

Fortunately for Slug-Man, Paige-o-tron is stupid.

Is that a sweater sale going on at the county jail?

Yowza!

Foom!

DID I MENTION HER SENSE OF HUMOR?

YOU DON'T EVEN WANT TO **KNOW** WHAT I WOULD FIND FUNNY RIGHT NOW...

AMEND

31

WHY THE BIG SMILE?

GUESS.

WELL, LET'S SEE... YOU COULDN'T HAVE ACED A TEST... YOU COULDN'T HAVE GOTTEN A DATE FOR THE PROM... YOU COULDN'T HAVE FINISHED YOUR HOMEWORK EARLY...

AMEND

IT MUST BE SOMETHING STUPID LIKE MOM IS LETTING YOU COOK DINNER TONIGHT.

WHY THE BIG SCOWL?

GUESS.

WHATCHA DOING?

TRYING TO FIGURE OUT WHAT I WANT TO COOK FOR DINNER.

COOKING made E Z

I WANT TO MAKE SOMETHING SPECIAL. UNFORGETTABLE.

SOMETHING EVERYONE WILL BE TALKING ABOUT FOR YEARS TO COME.

COOKING

LIKE, SAY, LAST SUMMER'S BLACKENED EGG SALAD.

THINK DAD'LL SPRING FOR LOBSTERS?

COOKING made E.Z.

AMEND

DON'T GO IN THE KITCHEN.

WHY?

PAIGE IS COOKING DINNER.

AND SHE WANTS IT TO BE A SURPRISE? SHE WANTS IT TO BE A SECRET?

UM, SHE JUST KINDA WANTS TO LIVE.

I SAID GET OUT!

MY FEET ARE STUCK.

AMEND

32

37

by Bill Amend

FoxTrot

HEY, PETE— WHATCHA DOING TODAY?

NOTHING. WHY?

FRED AND I WERE THINKING OF SQUEEZING IN A ROUND OF GOLF.

I FIGURED IF YOU HAD NOTHING ELSE PLANNED, YOU MIGHT WANT TO—...

JOIN YOU?!

IN A MANNER OF SPEAKING. MY DRIVER, PLEASE.

NOT ANOTHER PAR FIVE!

DAD, I THINK YOU NEED MORE CLUB.

SON, PLEASE. I THINK I KNOW WHAT I'M DOING.

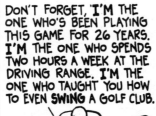

DON'T FORGET, I'M THE ONE WHO'S BEEN PLAYING THIS GAME FOR 26 YEARS. I'M THE ONE WHO SPENDS TWO HOURS A WEEK AT THE DRIVING RANGE. I'M THE ONE WHO TAUGHT YOU HOW TO EVEN SWING A GOLF CLUB.

.........SPLASH!

DON'T FORGET I'M THE ONE STUCK LOOKING FOR YOUR BALL.

MAYBE IT BOUNCED OUT...

WHAT DO YOU THINK? A BREAK TO THE LEFT?

RIGHT.

PUTT

NEXT TIME, SAY "CORRECT."

I'LL GO GET YOUR SAND WEDGE.

YOU SEE, PETER, A GOOD GOLF SHOT REQUIRES TOTAL AND SURE CONCENTRATION.

A BARKING DOG, A HONKING HORN, EVEN THE SNAP OF A TWIG CAN CAUSE A SHOT TO GO WILD.

IT'S A GAME OF NERVES AND I'D APPRECIATE YOUR COOPERATION.

SO SHOULD I COUGH DURING FRED'S BACKSWING OR DOWNSWING?

BOTH, IDEALLY.

OK, PETE, THIS IS IT. THE 18TH HOLE. THE PRESSURE COOKER.

WHAT'S THE SCORE?

LET'S SEE...FRED'S GOT AN 81 AND YOU'VE GOT AN 80.

WHOOPS—THAT'S 180.

BUT THEN, WHO LIKES PRESSURE ANYWAY?

NOT FRED, APPARENTLY.

ROGER, WHY DON'T YOU GO FIRST...

PETER, YOU REALLY CAME THROUGH FOR ME TODAY.

YOU CARRIED MY CLUBS... YOU GAVE ME ADVICE... YOU FOUND ALL BUT THREE OF MY BALLS...

A MAN COULDN'T ASK FOR A BETTER CADDY.

LET'S NOT RUIN IT NOW.

FIVE CENTS A **HOLE**?! ARE YOU **NUTS**?!

42

WELL, HERE WE ARE.

YUP.

WELL, THERE WE WERE.

YUP.

WELL, SCHOOL'S OVER.

YUP.

NO MORE CLASSES... NO MORE HOMEWORK...

NOPE.

NO MORE QUIZZES... NO MORE TESTS...

NOPE.

NO MORE GRUBBING FOR GRADES... NO MORE PETTY COMPETITION...

NOPE.

I MISS IT ALREADY.

RACE YOU TO THAT TREE...

WELL, MOM, I'VE DECIDED WHAT I WANT TO DO WITH MYSELF THIS SUMMER. OH?

IT'S GONNA BE TOUGH. IT'S GONNA BE PAINFUL. BUT I'M GONNA BITE THE BULLET, ROLL UP MY SLEEVES AND WORK...

WORK?! YOU'RE GOING TO WORK?!

AMEND

...OUT AND BECOME A CONTESTANT ON "AMERICAN GLADIATORS." WHY DO YOU GET YOUR STUPID HOPES UP LIKE THIS?!

MOM, PLEASE. IT'S GONNA BE HARD ENOUGH AS IT IS. I'M TALKING TO MYSELF.

WHAT ARE YOU DOING? PUSH-UPS.

PUSH-UPS? THE KEY TO DOING WELL IN "AMERICAN GLADIATORS" IS UPPER-BODY STRENGTH. THESE'LL GET MY TRICEPS, MY PECS AND MY DELTS IN SHAPE.

AMEND

PUSH-UPS? YES, PUSH-UPS. YOU GOT A PROBLEM WITH THAT?

I HAVE A PROBLEM WITH YOUR USING THE PLURAL. I'LL HAVE YOU KNOW I DID THREE BEFORE YOU CAME IN HERE.

I'VE HEARD THERE'S AN EVENT IN "AMERICAN GLADIATORS" CALLED "ASSAULT." UH HUH.

MEGA MASS 8000

WHERE YOU HAVE THIS BIG CANNON FIRING AT YOU AND YOU HAVE TO DODGE THE BULLETS. UH HUH.

AMEND

MEGA MASS 8000

I THOUGHT I MIGHT HELP YOU PRACTICE. THERE'S ALSO AN EVENT CALLED "THE ELIMINATOR"...

MEGA MASS 8000

"AMERICAN GLADIATORS"? ISN'T THAT THE SHOW WITH THE 300-POUND GOLIATHS?

YUP.

WHERE CONTESTANTS ARE PUMMELED TO PIECES BY THESE MONSTERS FOR AN HOUR UNTIL ONE PERSON LIMPS BATTERED AND BLOODY ACROSS THE FINISH LINE? AND IT'S ON TV ALL ACROSS THE COUNTRY?

BASIC-ALLY, YEAH.

AND YOU REALLY WANT TO DO THIS?

ABSO-LUTELY.

THANK YOU.

OF COURSE, YOU'D SEE IT LIVE.

WHY'S PETER ON THE ROOF?

HE'S PRACTICING FOR "THE WALL."

THE WHAT?

IT'S SOME EVENT ON "AMERICAN GLADIATORS" WHERE YOU HAVE TO SCALE A 25-FOOT CLIFF IN UNDER A MINUTE. HE HAS THIS FANTASY THAT HE'S GOING TO BE A CONTESTANT ON THE SHOW.

WHAM!

YOU MEAN, **HAD** A FANTASY.

I THOUGHT THAT TOO, BUT HE KEEPS GETTING UP.

WELL, GOODBYE "AMERICAN GLADIATORS."

WHAT'S WRONG?

I HURT MY BACK.

FALLING OFF THE ROOF, I'LL BET.

NO.

LIFTING ALL THOSE WEIGHTS?

NO.

TRYING TO DO 50 ONE-FINGER PUSH-UPS?

NO.

CRAWLING UP THE STAIRS BACKWARD WITH A NERF BALL IN YOUR MOUTH?

FLEXING IN FRONT OF A MIRROR.

OUCH.

47

WHATCHA DOING?

FIGURING OUT HOW I'M GONNA TALK MOM AND DAD INTO BUYING ME ONE OF THE NEW SUPER NINTENDO UNITS.

GOOD LUCK.

WHAT DO YOU THINK— SHOULD I STRESS THE IMPROVED CIRCUITRY AND GRAPHICS OR RATHER THE RECENT PRICE REDUCTIONS?

JASON, WHAT'S WRONG WITH YOUR OLD NINTENDO MACHINE?

UM, INTERESTING YOU SHOULD ASK.

WHAT DID YOU DO TO IT?!

YOU KNOW, MAYBE I SHOULDN'T BRING UP "CIRCUITRY"...

WHAT HAPPENED TO YOUR NINTENDO MACHINE?!

I KINDA KICKED IT.

JASON!

BUT I WOULDN'T HAVE KICKED IT IF I HADN'T BEEN IN A FIT OF RAGE! AND I WOULDN'T HAVE BEEN IN A FIT OF RAGE IF YOU HADN'T PULLED THE PLUG IN THE MIDDLE OF MY BEST MARIO BROTHERS GAME EVER!

I WOULDN'T HAVE PULLED THE PLUG IF YOU'D PUT IT ON "PAUSE" AND COME TO DINNER AS I ASKED.

OH, FINE. PASS THE BUCK.

YOU KNOW, I WISH I COULD FEEL BAD ABOUT THIS.

I, UM, STUMBLED ACROSS THIS AD FOR THE NEW SUPER NINTENDO...

TALK ABOUT DISILLUSIONING.

WHAT?

I ALWAYS ASSUMED THAT LIFE WAS GOOD. THAT LIFE WAS FAIR. THAT LIFE TOOK CARE OF KIDS LIKE ME.

AND?

I ACCIDENTALLY SMASHED MY NINTENDO MACHINE AND MOM AND DAD WON'T BUY ME A NEW ONE.

THERE IS NO GOD.

YOU KNOW, SOME MIGHT ARGUE—...

MOM, I'VE GOT A PROBLEM. SPRINGSTEEN AND U2 ARE BOTH ON TOUR THIS SUMMER.

AND?

AND AS MUCH AS I'D DO **ANYTHING** TO SEE THEM LIVE, I PROBABLY WON'T BE ABLE TO AFFORD TO GO.

...ON MY CURRENT MEAGER ALLOWANCE, THAT IS.

SO GET A JOB.

OK, AS MUCH AS I'D DO **ALMOST** ANYTHING...

YOU KNOW, YOU **DO** HAVE A PROBLEM.

MMM. BANANA.

MMM. CHOCOLATE.

THERE'S NO WAY YOUR CHOCOLATE IS AS GOOD AS THIS BANANA.

THERE'S NO WAY YOUR BANANA IS AS GOOD AS THIS CHOCOLATE.

I SUPPOSE THERE'S ONLY ONE WAY TO SETTLE THIS.

YOU KNOW, THAT RASPBERRY LOOKED PRETTY GOOD TOO...

BUT NOT **NEARLY** AS GOOD AS THE VANILLA...

THINK, ROGER, THINK.

YOU CAN'T LET HER WIN LIKE THIS.

THERE'S GOT TO BE **SOMETHING** YOU HAVEN'T TRIED.

SUPER **DUPER** PRETTY PLEASE??

ROGER, I **DON'T** WANT TO PLAY CHESS, OK?!

WHAT DO YOU SAY WE RENT "NIGHT ON BLOOD MOUNTAIN"?

VIDEOS 'R' US

RDR

OOO—FORGET **THAT**. LET'S GET "CORPSES DELECTI"!

JASON, REMEMBER THIS IS MOM'S MONEY WE'RE USING.

RDR

GOOD THINKING. LET'S GET BOTH.

YOU KNOW, I NEVER SAW "CADDYSHACK" IV THROUGH VII...

RDR

AMEND

ZZZZ...

PAIGE, WAKE UP! YOU'RE COVERED WITH WORMS!

HUH?

AMEND

AAAAA!

MORE SPAGHETTI, PLEASE.

JASON, YOU'RE A **TWIG**—WHERE DO YOU PUT IT?!

WHY DO WE HAVE FIREWORKS ON THE FOURTH OF JULY?

WELL...

FIREWORKS HAVE BEEN AROUND SINCE THE ANCIENT CHINESE. THEY'VE LONG BEEN USED TO COMMEM-ORATE HOLIDAYS, VICTORIES AND OTHER IMPORTANT DATES.

AMERICANS SET THEM OFF ON THE FOURTH OF JULY TO CELEBRATE THE SIGNING OF THE DECLARATION OF INDEPENDENCE.

AMEND

NO, WHY DO **WE** HAVE FIREWORKS?...

UM, PETER, YOU MIGHT WANT TO GRAB THAT HOSE.

53

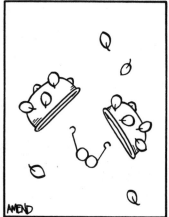

by Bill Amend

FoxTrot

Buy me.

IT'S LAME, BUT I'LL TAKE IT.

MOST EXCELLENT.

Jason Fox's Amazing FLIP-BOOKS $25⁰⁰ each

FLIP FLIP FLIP

CAN I PAY YOU AGAIN FOR THIS ONE?

FLIP FLIP FLIP

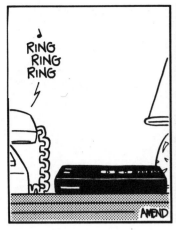

♪ RING RING RING

(CLICK) HELLO AND WELCOME TO THE JASON FOX HOTLINE— YOUR 24-HOUR SOURCE FOR ALL THINGS JASON.

FOR BREAKFAST TODAY, I HAD CHEERIOS AND—...

WHY DOES EVERY-ONE ALWAYS SOUND SO DARN GROUCHY ON THIS THING?

MUST BE THE TAPE.

I SAY IT'S A GIANT PIGEON.

I SAY IT'S A PTERO-DACTYL.

I SAY IT'S A GIANT PIGEON.

I SAY IT'S A PTERO-DACTYL.

LET'S JUST CALL IT "TROUBLE."

WELL, TIME TO SCRAM.

TWO WORDS, MOM: "SISTINE CHAPEL."

ARE THE FINS OK?

60

LAST ONE IN'S A STUPID MORON!

SCREECH!

KER-SPLASH!

AIEEE!

OR WAS THAT "FIRST ONE IN"?...

T-T-T-TOWEL, P-P-P-PLEASE...

61

JASON, WILL YOU PLEASE GO WAKE UP PAIGE? SHE'S BEEN ON THAT COUCH ALL AFTERNOON.

WITH PLEASURE.

CLINK

CLINK

...AND WITH QUINCY.

I'LL JUST, UM, WATCH FROM UP HERE IF YOU DON'T MIND.

MA ANDS AHR TREMBLANG...

OOO— PIERRE...

MA SPAHN ES TINGLANG...

OOO— PIERRE...

MY SKIN IS CRAWLING...

TWO MINUTES. WOW—THIS MIGHT BE A RECORD.

ZZZZ... OOO— PIERRE...

PAIGE, I'M SORRY YOU HAVE AN IGUANA ON YOUR FACE.

BUT IT'S DINNER TIME AND WE COULDN'T GET YOU TO WAKE UP ANY OTHER WAY.

NOW JUST TRY TO STAY CALM...

...AND LET GO OF YOUR BROTHER.

Please.

FIRST THINGS FIRST...

63

NOW I KNOW SOME OF YOU MIGHT BE WONDERING, "THE **DESERT**?! IN **AUGUST**?! HAS DAD LOST HIS **MIND**?!"...

I'M NOT WONDERING.

I'M NOT WONDERING.

ARE THESE REAL RATTLERS?

AND TELL THEM WHERE THEY'LL BE **STAYING**, ROGER...

I CAN'T BELIEVE WE'RE GOING **CAMPING**!

...IN THE **DESERT**!

...IN THE MIDDLE OF **AUGUST**!

WEIRDOS.

YOU KNOW, COWBOY GEAR MIGHT BE MORE APPROPRIATE...

LISTEN TO THIS, ANDY...

"CACTUS FLATS WAS ORIGINALLY HOME TO THE MUCKATOO INDIAN TRIBE UNTIL THEY ALL DIED OF HEAT STROKE."

I'LL BET WE FIND ARROWHEADS.

CAN'T YOU JUST GO **ALONE**?

LET ME SEE IF I'VE GOT THIS STRAIGHT...

YOU'RE GOING TO BE SLEEPING IN TENTS... ABOUT A ZILLION MILES FROM NOWHERE...

IN A DESERT FULL OF SNAKES, LIZARDS, SCORPIONS, TARANTULAS, BLACK WIDOWS AND MOUNTAIN LIONS.

BASICALLY, YES.

COOL.

OF COURSE, PAIGE WILL BE THERE.

PAIGE, C'MON— WE'RE ONLY GOING FOR TWO WEEKS! HOW BAD CAN IT BE?

THIS JUST IN...

RECORD HEAT HAS STRUCK THE DESERT COMMUNITY OF CACTUS FLATS, ARIZONA.

LET'S GO LIVE TO CORRESPONDENT PETER ARNETT WHO IS NOW IN CACTUS FLATS, PETER?

BERNIE, IT'S TOO HOT HERE. I QUIT.

FOURTEEN DAYS! IT'LL GO LIKE **THAT**!

SNAP!

MEANWHILE, IN POLITICS...

TWO WEEKS CAMPING IN THE DESERT?!

TWO WEEKS CAMPING IN THE DESERT?!

WHAT THE HECK AM I SUPPOSED TO PACK FOR TWO WEEKS CAMPING IN THE DESERT?!

THINK I'LL BLEND IN?

...BESIDES A SHOT GUN.

I ALSO GOT THESE...

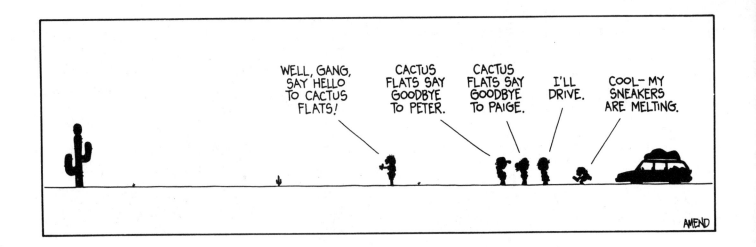

68

by Bill Amend

FOXTROT

LET'S SEE...
THERE'S RIGEL...
AND THERE'S
ARCTURUS...

THAT BIG STREAK,
OF COURSE, IS THE
MILKY WAY...

THERE'S THE
BIG DIPPER...
THERE'S THE
LITTLE DIPPER...

THERE'S ORION...
THERE'S DRACO...

THERE'S DENEB IN
THE CONSTELLATION
CYGNUS...

THERE'S VEGA... THERE'S
ANTARES... THERE'S THE
M13 GLOBULAR CLUSTER...

AND THERE, BROTHER PETER, IS
THE M51 GALAXY— SITE OF THE
MUCH PUBLICIZED "MYSTERY X"
AND SUSPECTED BLACK HOLE.

KINDA IRONIC
THAT WE'RE SO
BUTT-LOST.

MAYBE IF A CERTAIN SOMEONE HADN'T
KILLED THE FLASHLIGHT PLAYING "MR.
SPECTER-FACE"...

70

72

I'D **LIKE** TO SAY IT'S GOOD TO BE BACK.

NOW **THESE** CAN WAIT TILL TOMORROW.

SEPTEMBER

AMEND

WHO WAS ALBERT EINSTEIN!

OH, MY. IT LOOKS LIKE **NONE** OF YOU GOT THE FINAL JEOPARDY QUESTION RIGHT.

AMEND

WHO WAS ALBERT EINSTEIN!

AND YOU EACH BET EVERYTHING— SO **NO** ONE WINS THE $100,000 TOURNAMENT OF CHAMPIONS!

WHO WAS ALBERT EINSTEIN!

WHAT A SHAME.

WHO WAS ALEX TREBEK...

THE CORRECT RESPONSE, OF COURSE, WOULD HAVE BEEN, "WHO WAS ALBERT EINSTEIN."

WELL, ANDY, I THINK THIS'LL BE OUR LAST BARBECUE OF THE SEASON.

WHY'S THAT?

WELL, WHILE WE'RE NOT OUT OF CHARCOAL AND WE'RE NOT OUT OF LIGHTER FLUID...

...WE ARE OUT OF WARNINGS.

LARRY, GET THAT TANKER OVER HERE!

AMEND

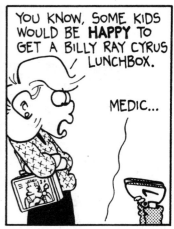

IT'S A MEDICAL MIRACLE, MOTHER! I'VE AGED SEVEN YEARS IN MY SLEEP!

UH-HUH.

IT'S TRUE! LOOK— I'VE EVEN GROWN A MUSTACHE! THE ONLY THING WE CAN DO AT THIS POINT IS TAKE ME OUT OF FIFTH GRADE AND ENROLL ME IN TWELFTH, WHERE I CAN STUDY CALCULUS, PHYSICS AND OTHER TOPICS MORE SUITED TO MY NOW-17-YEAR-OLD BRAIN.

YOUR MUSTACHE IS UPSIDE-DOWN.

WHY, IT'S, UM, ANOTHER MEDICAL MIRACLE!

SO HOW WAS THE FIRST DAY OF SCHOOL?

TRÉS STIMULATING.

OH? WHAT'D YOU LEARN?

THAT HUNKY BOBBY McALLISTER IS IN MY ENGLISH CLASS.

ANYTHING ELSE?

THAT HUNKY MIKEY SMITH IS IN MY GEOGRAPHY CLASS.

ANYTHING ELSE?

...OR WAS THAT GEOMETRY CLASS? LET ME CHECK MY NOTES...

MAY I HELP YOU?

I THINK THE COMPUTER GOOFED UP MY SCHEDULE.

OH?

WELL, LOOK: "PERIOD ONE, MATH... PERIOD THREE, MATH... PERIOD SIX, MATH..."

YOU'VE GOT ME IN FOUR MATH CLASSES!

UM, NEXT...

OR IS IT FIVE?...

MATH HOMEWORK...

SCIENCE HOMEWORK...

HALLELUJAH!

APPROPRIATE MUSIC ON THE STEREO...

MUST YOU DO THIS EVERY YEAR?

$$25\overline{)500} = \sqrt{400} = 5^2 - 5^1 = \frac{d}{dx}20x = (-5i)(4i)$$

$$= 40\sin\frac{\pi}{6} = \int_0^2 10x\,dx = \frac{5!}{3!} = \ln e =$$

THREE MONTHS OF THERAPY... GONE.

READ!

WELL, I FINISHED MY HOMEWORK.

ALL OF IT?

YUP.

FOR THE WHOLE WEEKEND?

FOR THE WHOLE YEAR.

EXCUSE ME, I HAVE TO GO MELD WITH THE TV NOW...

CALENDAR YEAR OR SCHOOL YEAR?

KIDS, I'M EXHAUSTED.

WOULD ANYONE MIND IF WE JUST WENT OUT AND GOT SOME BURGERS FOR DINNER?

POW!

WHEN YOU FINALLY GET UP, PLEASE EXPLAIN TO PAIGE THE "DIBS-ON-THE-FRONT-SEAT-TWO-DAY-CARRY-OVER RULE."

WAIT FOR ME!

DID I MENTION I WAS EXHAUSTED?

CAN I HELP YOU?

WELL, LET'S SEE...

WE'LL TAKE FIVE CHEESE-BURGERS...

I DON'T WANT CHEESE ON MINE!

I DON'T WANT MAYONNAISE!

I DON'T WANT PICKLES OR MAYONNAISE!

I WANT A HOT DOG!

I DON'T WANT ONIONS!

I DON'T WANT TOMATOES!

I DON'T WANT MUSTARD!

I WANT A HOT DOG!

ONE FAMILY SPECIAL...

CAN WE START OVER?

OOO— "GARFIELD" CUPS...

COULD I HAVE SOME EXTRA KETCHUP PACKETS?

COULD I HAVE SOME EXTRA MUSTARD PACKETS?

COULD I HAVE SOME EXTRA RELISH PACKETS?

COULD I HAVE ONE OF THOSE PLASTIC SALAD FORKS?

HEE HEE HEE...

WHAT'S SO FUNNY?

TOMORROW'S MY DAY TO BRING SOMETHING FOR SHOW AND TELL.

YEAH, SO?

I'M BRINGING QUINCY. THE GIRLS ARE ALL GONNA HAVE HEART ATTACKS.

YOU DON'T KNOW ANYTHING ABOUT LIABILITY LAW, DO YOU?

YOU KNOW, MOST KIDS JUST BRING STAMP COLLECTIONS...

WHAT'S IN THE BOX?

I'M BRINGING QUINCY TO SCHOOL FOR SHOW AND TELL.

Live Animal

MISS O'MALLEY **SAID** YOU COULD?

Live Animal

I MEAN, YOU DID **ASK**, RIGHT?

DIDN'T WE GO THROUGH THIS LAST YEAR WITH YOUR TICK FARM?

WAS IT **MY** FAULT THEY GOT LOOSE?!

WHY, JASON, **YOU'RE** HERE EARLY.

MISS O'MALLEY?

Live Animal Read!

MY MOM WANTED ME TO DISCUSS MY SHOW AND TELL PRESENTATION WITH YOU BEFORE CLASS STARTS.

WHY'S THAT?

WELL, I BROUGHT MY PET IGUANA, QUINCY, AND HE TENDS TO BE SOMETHING OF A HANDFUL.

AND SO SHE WANTED MY PERMISSION?

A REGULAR CARL LEWIS, I SEE.

INDEMNIFICATION.

Live Animal Read!

AAAA!

WHY, MISS O'MALLEY, YOU SEEM FRIGHTENED.

AAAA!

WHY, MISS O'MALLEY, YOU SEEM TERRIFIED.

AAAA!

WHY, MISS O'MALLEY, YOU SEEM DOWNRIGHT PETRIFIED.

AAAA! HE'S SO CUTE!

WHY, MISS O— WHAT?!

YOU THINK QUINCY'S CUTE?!

JASON, HE'S DARLING!

GOOCHY, GOOCHY, GOOCHY...

AND YOU'RE A GIRL?!

SO I'VE BEEN TOLD.

OOO, LOOK— HE'S THUMPING!

SOMETHING IS GOING DRASTICALLY, DREADFULLY WRONG HERE.

TALK ABOUT NIGHTMARES.

SHOW AND TELL?

I NEVER EVEN MADE IT TO SHOW AND TELL! I WENT IN EARLY TO SHOW QUINCY TO MISS O'MALLEY LIKE YOU TOLD ME TO...

AND HE SCARED HER HALF TO DEATH?

SHE GAVE HIM A TUMMY RUB!

I SPENT THE DAY ILL IN THE NURSE'S OFFICE.

I TAKE IT I'LL BE GETTING ANOTHER ONE OF THOSE LETTERS...

84

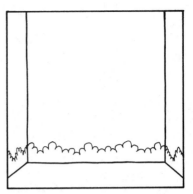

FoxTrot

by Bill Amend

TA DA! ♫

HELLO, BOYS AND GIRLS. MY NAME IS MR. DRAGS AND I AM JASON'S FALL SEMESTER CRAFT PROJECT.

ALLOW ME TO DEMONSTRATE MY MYRIAD TALENTS.

WHEN JASON PULLS THIS STRING, I MOVE MY TAIL.

WHEN JASON PULLS THESE STRINGS, I FLAP MY WINGS.

WHEN JASON PULLS **THIS** STRING...

CLICK

MIND YOU, THE KIDS AT SCHOOL WILL BE SEATED FARTHER BACK.

OH, GOOD.

AMEND

85

Beep Beep
Beep Beep
Beep Beep
Beep

Beep Beep
Beep Beep
Beep Beep
Beep

MOM, IS IT OK IF I USE YOUR OFFICE PHONE THIS MORNING?

WHY?

SPRINGSTEEN TICKETS GO ON SALE AT 10 AND IT JUST OCCURRED TO ME THAT YOUR PHONE HAS A SPEED DIALER.

THAT'S FINE. I HAVE TO GO RUN SOME ERRANDS ANYWAY.

YEE-HA!

WHAT THE—...

MOOD MUSIC.

I'VE GOT "BORN TO RUN" BLASTING ON THE STEREO FOR GOOD LUCK...

I'VE GOT MY SPRINGSTEEN RECORDS, TAPES AND CDs ERECTED INTO A SHRINE-O-BRUCE FOR GOOD LUCK...

I'VE GOT THE TICKET-MASTER PHONE NUMBER PROGRAMMED INTO MEMORY BUTTON SEVEN FOR GOOD LUCK...

AND WILL YOU LOOK AT THAT SUNRISE.

PAY NO ATTENTION TO THE GIRL WITH THE BASEBALL BAT.

Beep Beep
Beep Beep
Beep Beep
Beep

SPRINGSTEEN TICKETS GO ON SALE TOMORROW.

YOU REALLY THINK PRACTICE WILL HELP?

ICE

FEAST YOUR EYES ON THE WORLD'S NEXT MULTI-BIJILLIONAIRE.

OH?

MY SCHOOL IS STARTING A MONTHLY NEWSPAPER AND I VOLUNTEERED TO DO A COMIC STRIP. I'M GONNA BE RICH.

JASON, "VOLUNTEERING" MEANS YOU'RE DOING IT FOR FREE.

I'M ONLY DOING THE STRIP FOR FREE.

WELL, WHAT ELSE IS THERE?

A LITTLE THING CALLED MERCHANDISING. EVER HEARD OF "GARFIELD"?

YOU KNOW, FOR ONCE I'D LIKE TO BE ABLE TO ATTEND A PTA MEETING...

I'VE GOT IT ALL FIGURED OUT.

I'M GOING TO HAVE COFFEE MUGS BASED ON MY COMIC STRIP... T-SHIRTS BASED ON MY COMIC STRIP... PLUSH TOYS BASED ON MY COMIC STRIP AND AN ASSORTMENT OF ALL-OCCASION GIFT WRAP BASED ON MY COMIC STRIP.

WHAT'S YOUR STRIP ABOUT?

OK, I'VE GOT IT MOSTLY FIGURED OUT.

MAYBE IF YOU TOOK A POLL?

PAIGE, THIS IS UNBELIEVABLE. I'M GONNA NEED LAWYERS... BUSINESS ADVISERS...

TRADE EXPERTS... LITERARY AGENTS... PLUSH-TOY DESIGNERS... DIRECT-MAIL SPECIALISTS... PRIMARY AND SECONDARY MARKET SUPPORT... LOTS OF ACCOUNTANTS...

JASON, YOU'RE DRAWING A COMIC STRIP FOR YOUR STUPID SCHOOL NEWSPAPER!

PENCILS... PENS...

ASPIRIN...

MOM, I'M HAVING TROUBLE DECIDING ON A CENTRAL CHARACTER FOR MY COMIC STRIP.

NO ONE SAID IT'D BE EASY.

DOG CHARACTERS HAVE BEEN EXPLOITED AND MERCHANDISED TO DEATH... CAT CHARACTERS HAVE BEEN EXPLOITED AND MERCHANDISED TO DEATH... MOUSE CHARACTERS HAVE BEEN EXPLOITED AND MERCHANDISED TO DEATH...

MAYBE I SHOULD HAVE ONE OF EACH...

YOU KNOW, HUMANS CAN BE FUNNY, TOO.

AMEND

HONESTLY, WHAT DO YOU THINK OF MY COMIC STRIP?

WELL, IT'S NOT PARTICULARLY FUNNY...

AND IT'S NOT PARTICULARLY WELL-DRAWN...

IN FACT, IT'S PROBABLY THE LAMEST THING I'VE EVER SEEN.

MY, BUT YOU DO HAVE PURE MOTIVES...

BUT WILL IT SELL T-SHIRTS?

AMEND

DO YOU THINK THE WORLD IS READY FOR CARTOON-SHAPED TY-D-BOL TABLETS?

JASON, PLEASE.

WHAT DO YOU MEAN?

CAN'T YOU DO A COMIC STRIP JUST FOR THE FUN OF IT?! WHAT EVER HAPPENED TO ART FOR ART'S SAKE?!

YOUR SCHOOL NEWSPAPER IS GIVING YOU A CHANCE TO EXPLORE WHAT SHOULD BE A WONDERFUL CREATIVE OUTLET AND YOU'RE TWISTING IT INTO SOME CYNICAL SCAM TO GET RICH QUICK! I DON'T WANT TO HEAR ANOTHER WORD ABOUT CARTOON MERCHANDISE. CAPEESH?

FOR THE RECORD, A GOOD SCAM IS ART.

ACTUALLY, THESE ARE KINDA CUTE...

AMEND

YOU'RE UP EARLY.

TODAY'S THE DAY THE SCHOOL NEWSPAPER COMES OUT.

WITH, I HASTEN TO ADD, THE FIRST INSTALLMENT OF MY COMIC STRIP...

"SQUISHY AND SQUASHY, THE TALKING ROADKILL BROTHERS."

AMEND

WANTED A HEAD START OUT OF TOWN, I GATHER.

SHOULD I SIGN AUTOGRAPHS WITH A BLACK PEN OR BLUE?

WHAT'S WITH THE SUNGLASSES?

CELEBRITIES ALWAYS WEAR SUNGLASSES.

NOW THAT MY COMIC STRIP RUNS IN THE SCHOOL NEWSPAPER, I HAVE TO MAINTAIN A CERTAIN AIR OF SOPHISTICATED COOLNESS.

AMEND

UM...

SO WHAT PAGE DID THEY PUT ME ON?

Flip Flip Flip

UM...

DID I PASS IT? IT'S HARD TO READ WITH THESE GLASSES...

AAAA! WHY ISN'T MY COMIC STRIP IN HERE?!

I WAS GOING TO ASK YOU THE SAME QUESTION.

I DON'T GET IT — I DREW IT THE RIGHT SIZE... I TURNED IT IN ON TIME...

I DOUBLE-CHECKED ALL MY SPELLING AND PUNCTUATION...

THAT'S RIGHT— YOU ASKED ME IF "GROSS DISMEMBERMENT" WAS HYPHENATED.

AMEND

GOOD THING, TOO. I USED THE TERM 19 TIMES.

HERE COMES THE PRINCIPAL. MAYBE HE WOULD KNOW.

MR. MARTINI, MY COMIC STRIP WAS SUPPOSED TO BE IN THE SCHOOL PAPER!

IT'S NOT ON PAGE ONE... IT'S NOT ON PAGE TWO... IT'S NOT ON PAGE THREE...

Flip
Flip
Flip

WHAT HAPPENED TO MY COMIC STRIP?!

LET'S JUST SAY "SQUISHY AND SQUASHY, THE TALKING ROADKILL BROTHERS" MET YET ANOTHER DEATH.

BUT HOW?! THEY WERE SECRETLY VAMPIRES!

JASON, YOU HAVE TO UNDERSTAND. WE'RE TALKING ABOUT A SCHOOL NEWSPAPER.

MY RIGHTS HAVE BEEN SQUASHED!

JASON, JUST BECAUSE YOU SUBMITTED A COMIC STRIP, IT DOESN'T MEAN WE'RE OBLIGATED TO RUN IT.

MY RIGHTS HAVE BEEN SQUISHED!

MY RIGHTS HAVE BEEN SQUISHED AND SQUASHED AND TRAMPLED AND—...

COULD YOU MAYBE, UM, USE SOME LESS-COLORFUL LANGUAGE?

I MEAN, HAVE YOU EVER SEEN SUCH WELL-DRAWN ROADKILL?...

SO WHAT'S THE STORY WITH YOUR COMIC STRIP?

THE STORY IS THAT CENSORSHIP IS ALIVE AND WELL IN THIS COUNTRY.

OH, SURE, THE SCHOOL NEWSPAPER WILL PRINT YOUR STUFF IF IT'S SAFE... IF IT'S INOFFENSIVE... IF IT'S PABLUM...

BUT SUBMIT SOMETHING A LITTLE DIFFERENT... SOMETHING THAT CHALLENGES THE READER... SOMETHING PEOPLE MIGHT DARE TALK ABOUT AND YOU MIGHT AS WELL KISS IT GOODBYE FROM THE START!

I WONDER IF THEY KNOW THE LESSON THEY'RE TEACHING.

MAYBE IF MY ROADKILL CHARACTERS TOLD HAPPY JOKES...

Please use each of the following words in a sentence:

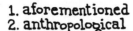

1. aforementioned
2. anthropological
3. brevity
4. cusp
5. credenza
6. dogmatic

45. unilateral
46. vaward
47. vestige
48. whet
49. xenograft
50. yaw

THIS IS GONNA BE ONE DOOZY OF A SENTENCE...

HEY, PAIGE — THAT WAS PRETTY CLEVER HOW YOU LIED TO MOM ABOUT WHERE YOU WENT LAST NIGHT.

I MEAN, YOU DID **LIE**, RIGHT?

RIGHT??

MAYBE HIDING THE MIKE IN A BOUTONNIERE **WASN'T** SUCH A GOOD IDEA.

WHAT WAS ALL THAT SQUEALING NOISE?

RAKE RAKE RAKE

RAKE RAKE RAKE

RAKE RAKE RAKE

HOW'S IT GOING?

I CAN SEE MY FLOOR NOW...

NO TIME FOR BREAKFAST!

NO TIME FOR COFFEE!

WHAM!

TIME, HOWEVER, FOR ASPIRIN.

THE, UM, DOOR IS ON **THAT** WALL.

JASON, PLEASE — HALLOWEEN'S NOT FOR TWO MORE WEEKS.

JASON? MY NAME IS PAIGE.

PETER, PASS THE MASHED POTATOES.

UM, DAD, GET READY TO DUCK.

I THOUGHT THIS WAS CHICKEN...

BWAA-HA-HA-HA-HAA!...

HALLOWEEN IS COMING.

IN FOOTBALL TERMS, THAT WAS YOUR 2×10^4-MINUTE WARNING.

AND IN "NERDLY-BOY" TERMS...

FoxTrot

by Bill Amend

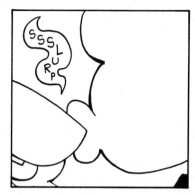

HEY, PETER, ARE YOU GOING TO THE BRUCE SPRINGSTEEN CONCERT ON SATURDAY?

NO. CAN YOU BELIEVE IT?!

I MEAN, **ME**—PETER "BORN TO RUN" FOX! I'D GIVE **ANYTHING** FOR A TICKET!

ANYTHING! ANYTHING! **ANYTHING!** JUST FOR ONE OF THOSE LITTLE PIECES OF PAPER THAT SAYS—...

"SECTION ONE, ROW SIX, SEAT H"?

MAN, FOR ROW SIX I'D REEEEEEALLY GIVE ANYTHING.

SO YOU'D GIVE ANYTHING FOR THIS, HMM?

HOW'D YOU GET A SPRINGSTEEN TICKET?!

THAT'S NOT IMPORTANT.

I'VE BEEN TRYING FOR WEEKS TO GET ONE! IT'S TOTALLY SOLD OUT!

I MEAN, I'M PRACTICALLY READY TO MAKE A DEAL WITH THE DEVIL!

SO MAKE A DEAL WITH YOUR SISTER.

YOU MEAN, A DEAL WITH AN ANGEL?

...AND AFTER YOU'VE WALLPAPERED MY ROOM, YOU CAN STEAM-CLEAN MY CARPET...

I'LL ALSO EXPECT YOU TO DRIVE ME TO AND FROM THE MALL EVERY SATURDAY AND SUNDAY FOR, OH, LET'S SAY SIX MONTHS...

PAIGE, ALL YOU'RE DOING IS GIVING ME A TICKET TO A STUPID BRUCE SPRINGSTEEN COG... COGPH... COMFLERT!

MAKE THAT **NINE** MONTHS...

STUPID DROOL.

PETER, DO YOU WANT THIS SPRINGSTEEN TICKET OR NOT?

PAIGE, YOU'RE ASKING TOO MUCH!

LOOK, I'LL DO YOUR HOMEWORK... I'LL CLEAN YOUR ROOM... I'LL DRIVE YOU TO AND FROM THE MALL... I'LL BUTTER YOUR TOAST ON SUNDAYS...

AMEND

BUT I WILL NOT ORDER VANITY LICENSE PLATES THAT SAY "ILUV210"!

YOU KNOW, I'LL BET IN ROW SIX YOU CAN COUNT BRUCE'S EARRINGS.

I'LL GET A BUMPER STICKER! PAIGE, PLEASE!

WELL, PETER, I THINK WE'VE WORKED OUT A PRETTY GOOD DEAL.

I AGREE.

YOU GET A SIXTH ROW BRUCE SPRINGSTEEN TICKET... I GET NINE MONTHS OF MISCELLANEOUS CHORES AND FAVORS OUT OF YOU... I'D SAY WE'RE BOTH WINNERS.

I AGREE.

HERE'S YOUR TICKET.

COME TO PAPPA, BABY, OH, BABY!...

NOT THAT SOME OF US AREN'T ALSO LOSERS.

IS IT ME, OR IS THIS THING GLOWING?

AMEND

YOU ARE LOOKING AT THE HAPPIEST KID ON EARTH RIGHT NOW.

NOTHING COULD BUM ME OUT. NOTHING COULD RUIN MY MOOD.

DID PAIGE GIVE YOU THE BRUCE SPRINGSTEEN TICKET I GOT FOR YOU?

AMEND

EXCUSE ME A MINUTE.

WHY DO YOU HAVE YOUR SISTER'S LAUNDRY?

WE HAD A MOCK PRESIDENTIAL ELECTION AT SCHOOL TODAY.

OH? WHO'D YOU VOTE FOR?

BILL CLINTON.

WHY'S THAT?

HE HAS A DAUGHTER MY AGE. I FIGURE HE UNDERSTANDS MY CONCERNS.

I CAN SEE HOW IT WOULD TAKE A RHODES SCHOLAR.

DOES THIS WATCHBAND MAKE MY NOSE LOOK BIG?

AMEND

HEY, PETER— GUESS WHAT I'M GONNA BE FOR HALLOWEEN.

HEY, MOM— GUESS WHAT I'M GONNA BE FOR HALLOWEEN.

AMEND

HEY, DAD— GUESS WHAT I'M GONNA BE FOR HALLOWEEN.

THE INVISIBLE MAN, APPARENTLY.

JASON, GO AWAY.

WHAT'S THIS?

A LIST OF THE STUFF I'LL NEED FOR HALLOWEEN.

MONSTER MAKEUP...
MONSTER CLOTHES...
MONSTER GLOVES...
MONSTER HAIR STUFF...
MONSTER SHOES...
MONSTER ACCESSORIES..

JASON, WHERE AM I SUPPOSED TO **GET** ALL THIS?

AMEND

MOM NEEDS TO KNOW WHERE YOU SHOP.

WHAT FOR?

I CAN'T WAIT FOR THIS ELECTION..

I MEAN, I **REALLY** CAN'T WAIT FOR THIS ELECTION.

I MEAN, I REALLY, REALLY, **REALLY**, REALLY CAN'T WAIT FOR THIS ELECTION.

AMEND

BECAUSE YOUR BOY'S GONNA WIN?

BECAUSE THESE COMMERCIALS WILL STOP.

Here's what Clinton economics could mean to your cat...

MAN, WHAT A WEEK. AM I GLAD TO BE HOME.

(CLICK)

AMEND

BOING! BOING! BOING!

...IN A TEMPERED AND EXTREMELY LIMITED SORT OF WAY.

DAD, YOU MISSED THE SECOND TRIP-WIRE!

I SCOOPED MY PUMPKIN OUT. NOW WHAT DO I DO?

SCOOPED IT OUT? I HOPE YOU PUT PAPER DOWN.

OF COURSE I PUT PAPER DOWN. LOTS OF PAPER. TONS OF PAPER. NICE, THICK SHEETS OF PAPER.

AMEND

AAAA! WHO PILED PUMPKIN GOOP ALL OVER MY HOMEWORK?!

I GUESS I **DO** KNOW WHAT TO DO NOW.

PAIGE, **DON'T!**

Why does Shakespeare echo this theme not once but <u>twice</u> in the third act?

What larger purpose do Hamlet's mood swings serve? And what, if anything, do Ophelia's flowers symbolize?

"HOW SHOULD **I** KNOW?" IS CERTAINLY AN **ORIGINAL** CONCLUSION...

SO IT'S GOOD?

MOM, CAN I GET MY OWN PHONE LINE?

NO. WHY?

WELL, YOU WOULDN'T HAVE TO WAIT FOR ME TO FINISH MY CALLS... YOU WOULDN'T HAVE TO TAKE MESSAGES FOR ME WHEN I'M NOT HOME... THIS NEW LINE WOULDN'T BE —...

...TAPPED!

PAIGE, PLEASE.

MEDIC...

I SUPPOSE YOU COULD JUST BUY ME A SHOT-GUN.

LOOK, KIDS...

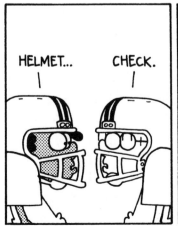
HELMET...

CHECK.

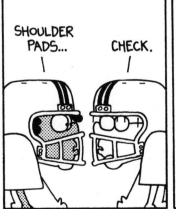
SHOULDER PADS...

CHECK.

DART GUNS...

CHECK.

Paige's Room Keep Out

ZZZZ...

I ♥ 210

105

FoxTrot

by Bill Amend

LET ME GUESS—IT'S MY WEEK TO RAKE.

WHY, NOW THAT YOU MENTION IT...

AMEND

MOM, CAN I HAVE AN ADVANCE ON MY ALLOWANCE, PLEASE PLEASE PLEASE?!

WHAT FOR?

MARCUS SAID THAT THIS MONTH'S CINEMAFANGIQUE MAGAZINE HAS A WHOLE PAGE OF UNAUTHORIZED BEHIND-THE-SCENES PHOTOS OF THE FILMING OF "JURASSIC PARK"!

HOW MUCH DOES IT COST?

AMEND

SO WHAT YOU MEANT TO ASK WAS, "CAN I HAVE QUITE A FEW ADVANCES ON MY ALLOWANCE."

FIVE DOLLARS.

MOM, PLEASE! THEY'LL SELL OUT TODAY, I KNOW IT!

DIDN'T WE GO THROUGH THIS WITH THE "GREATS OF ASTRONOMY" TRADING CARD SERIES?

PLEASE PLEASE PLEASE PLEASE PLEASE PLEASE PLEASE PLEASE PLEASE PLEASE PLEASE PLEASE PLEASE PLEASE

PLEASE PLEASE

PLEASE PLEASE PLEASE PLEASE PLEASE PLEASE PLEASE PLEASE PLEASE PLEASE PLEASE PLEASE PLEASE—...

FINE! HERE! JUST GO AWAY!

AMEND

WHO SAYS KIDS DON'T WORK FOR THEIR MONEY.

DO YOU HAVE THIS MONTH'S CINEMA-FANGIQUE MAGAZINE?

THE ONE WITH THE "JURASSIC PARK" PHOTOS? NOPE. ALL SOLD OUT.

Phaser Sale

WHAT?! NO! AAAA! I KNEW THIS WOULD HAPPEN!

Ask About our Dr.Who Sleepwear

Phaser Sale

(SOB) JUST KIDDING. SEE?— I'M WEARING MY STAR FLEET INSIGNIA UPSIDE-DOWN. THAT MEANS EVERYTHING I SAY MUST BE TREATED AS A LIE. DIDN'T YOU EVER READ "NEXT GENERATION" PAPERBACK #392: "THE OBSIDION PARADOX"?

THESE WOULDN'T HAPPEN TO WORK, WOULD THEY?

DOES PLASMA MAN BATHE IN NEUTRINO WATER?

AMEND

Phaser Sale

WOOO-OOO. BET YOU'RE JEALOUS.

OF WHAT?

THAT I HAVE THE NEW ISSUE OF CINEMAFANGIQUE MAGAZINE WITH A FULL PAGE OF UNAUTHORIZED BEHIND-THE-SCENES PHOTOS OF "JURASSIC PARK" BEING FILMED AND YOU DON'T.

YOU MUST BE INSANE.

LET'S JUST TAKE A PEEK TO SEE WHAT YOU'RE MISSING: "TOP: UNIDENTIFIED BLUR, THOUGHT TO BE STEVEN SPIELBERG, GIVES DIRECTION TO LARGER BLUR, THOUGHT TO BE T-REX ROBOT."

I HEAR THEY TOOK THESE FROM A SATELLITE.

UNIDENTIFIED BLUR, THOUGHT TO BE PAIGE MOVING OUT...

SO DID YOU GET YOUR MAGAZINE?

YUP. WANNA SEE?

SURE.

THE "JURASSIC PARK" PHOTOS ARE ON PAGE 27 RIGHT AFTER THE FULL-COLOR FOLD-OUT "HEROES OF THE KLINGON EMPIRE" COLLECTOR SERIES POSTER SUPPLEMENT.

I'M GLAD **YOU**, AT LEAST, RECOGNIZE JUST HOW COOL THESE BEHIND-THE-SCENES PHOTOS ARE. PETER, PAIGE AND DAD DIDN'T EVEN WANT TO LOOK AT THEM. LOSERS.

Now on video!!! Dragula

I JUST WANTED TO CHECK THE PRICE TO SEE IF YOU OWED ME ANY CHANGE.

AM I THE **ONLY** PERSON WITH A NORMAL INTEREST IN MOTION PICTURE DINOSAUR SPECIAL EFFECTS TECHNOLOGY?!

JASON, I'M SORRY IF I SEEMED INDIFFERENT. OF **COURSE** I WANT TO SEE YOUR DINOSAUR PHOTOS.

YOU'RE JUST HUMORING ME.

FINE. **DON'T** SHOW ME THE PHOTOS.

NOW YOU'RE JUST HUMORING MY ACCUSATION THAT YOU'RE HUMORING ME.

FINE. **SHOW** ME THE PHOTOS.

NOW YOU'RE JUST HUMORING MY ACCUSATION THAT YOU'RE HUMORING MY ACCUSATION THAT YOU'RE HUMORING ME.

BELIEVE ME, I'M RUNNING OUT OF HUMOR. **FAST.**

OK. NOW **THAT** HAS A CERTAIN CREDIBILITY...

FoxTrot

by Bill Amend

So, Raphael, what do you want to do today?

I don't know, Donatello. What do you want to do today?

We could do lots of things if only we had a Ninja Turtle Action Pump Lunar Lander Assault Vehicle.

So true.

Or a battery-operated, remote-controlled Ninja Turtle Dust Copter and Command Center.

Tell me about it.

Or a Deluxe Ninja Turtle Aqua Sub Activity Pack.

Like Marcus has.

Or, dare I mention it?...

The new Ninja Turtle Sewer Fortress Scale Model Construction Set with Realglo™ Laser Arsenal?

Why don't I tell you what to do.

You know, the dust copter will get me out of the house...

AMEND

WHERE'S MY WALLET?!

WHERE'S MY BRIEFCASE?!

WHERE'RE MY KEYS?!

WHERE'S THE FIRE?

HEE HEE... GOOD ONE, OFFICER...

SIR, I CLOCKED YOU GOING 45 IN A 25 MPH ZONE.

THERE MUST BE SOME MISTAKE.

SIR, I DON'T SEE HOW THERE **COULD** HAVE BEEN A MISTAKE.

RIP!

...ON MY PART.

$200?!
AAAA!

SLAM!

AAAARGH!

GRRRRRRRRR...

ASK ME HOW MY DAY WAS.

NOW, REMEMBER, I'M UNARMED...

FoxTrot
by Bill Amend

SO WHAT DO YOU WANT TO DO TODAY?

WELL, WE COULD GO...

...ALLIGATOR WRESTLING!

MOM, IS IT OK WITH YOU IF MARCUS AND I GO BUNGEE JUMPING?

OF COURSE NOT. NO.

WHAT ABOUT HANG GLIDING?

NO.

WHAT ABOUT PARACHUTING?

NO!

WHAT ABOUT CLIFF DIVING?

NO!

AMEND

WHAT ABOUT SHARK FEEDING?

DID IT EVER OCCUR TO YOU THAT I **MIGHT** BE TRYING TO **READ**?!

PERSONALLY, THAT KINDA CURED MY DEATH-LUST.

YOU KNOW, SHE DIDN'T SAY **NO**...

QUINCY SAYS YOU'RE UGLY.

QUINCY SAYS YOU'RE STUPID.

QUINCY SAYS HE'S SEEN SMOOTHER SKIN ON A PINEAPPLE.

IT'S ALWAYS THE **MESSENGER** THAT GETS IT.

LOOKS LIKE DAD'S GONNA BE UP WORKING ALL NIGHT.

WHY'S THAT?

HE BROUGHT HOME A LAPTOP COMPUTER.

SO? MAYBE HE JUST HAS TO CRUNCH A COUPLE OF NUMBERS.

THAT'S NOT THE POINT.

I KNOW THIS THING TURNS ON **SOME**HOW...

♪ NO MORE SCHOOL FOR FOUR DAYS...

♩ NO MORE SCHOOL FOR FOUR DAYS...

♩ NO MORE SCHOOL FOR—...

HAIL, PILGRIM!

SO MUCH FOR GIVING THANKS.

BY THE WAY, IT'S **FIVE** DAYS IF YOU COUNT TODAY.

ROGER, WHEN I SAID, "LET'S BOW OUR HEADS"...

PETER, WOULD IT BOTHER YOU IF I WENT OUT WITH OTHER BOYS ONCE IN A WHILE?

WHAT?!

YOU KNOW, IF I DATED OTHER GUYS.

DENISE, OF **COURSE** IT WOULD BOTHER ME!

HMMPH.

WHAT DO YOU **EXPECT** ME TO SAY?!

THAT IT WOULD **KILL** YOU! THAT IT WOULD **DEVASTATE** YOU! THAT IT WOULD FOREVER SCAR YOUR TORTURED **SOUL**!...

WELL, I MEANT "BOTHER" IN THAT SOUL-SCARRING WAY...

READ 'EM AND WEEP.

MAN...

PAIGE, DON'T YOU HAVE EIGHT TONS OF HOMEWORK YOU SHOULD BE DOING?

READ 'EM AND **REALLY** WEEP.

MAN...

NOTHING LIKE A NICE BIG BOWL OF SUGAR FROSTED HONEY FLAKES.

JASON, CUT IT OUT.

WHAT'D I DO?

WE HAVE TO DISSECT FROGS IN BIOLOGY TODAY. I'M QUEASY ENOUGH WITHOUT HAVING TO THINK OF FOOD.

I GUESS THE MILK COUNTS AS FOOD.

THAT BLUE STUFF IS **MILK**?!

AMEND

MOTHER, I CAN'T GO TO SCHOOL TODAY...

PAIGE, WHY NOT?

WE HAVE TO DISSECT FROGS IN BIOLOGY. IT'S JUST GONNA BE TOO GROSS FOR ME.

HAVING TO LOOK AT THEIR HEARTS... THEIR STOMACHS... THEIR INTESTINES...

THEIR PAIGE-SIZED BRAINS...

NOT THAT I WOULDN'T LOVE DISSECTING **SOME** THINGS...

JASON, SCRAM.

AMEND

SORRY. IT'S FOR SCIENCE.

^ ^ ERK.

SORRY. IT'S FOR SCIENCE.

PETER, TURN THE CAR AROUND! **PLEASE**?!

PAIGE, WE'RE GOING TO BE LATE FOR SCHOOL AS IT IS!

AMEND

OK, CLASS, YOU ALL HAVE YOUR FROGS.

IF THERE AREN'T ANY QUESTIONS, WE CAN BEGIN OUR DISSECTION AS DISCUSSED.

YES, PAIGE?

CAN I JUST GO TO THE NURSE'S OFFICE NOW AND SAVE ALL CONCERNED THE "MY GETTING SICK" PART?

PAIGE, TRY TO RELAX AND THINK OF IT AS SCIENCE.

I STILL MAY THROW UP.

HOW 'BOUT IF I HOLD YOUR HAND?

AMEND

I'M SORRY I HAVE TO CUT YOU UP, MR. FROG.

I'M SORRY I HAVE TO PEEL BACK YOUR SKIN AND POKE THROUGH YOUR INNARDS.

I'M SORRY I HAVE TO LABEL YOUR ORGANS AND SNIP OUT YOUR HEART.

BUT WE HAVE THIS THING CALLED A GRADE POINT AVERAGE...

THERE'S ALSO A THING CALLED AN HOUR HAND.

AMEND

OK, EVERYONE, LET'S MAKE OUR FIRST INCISION, BEGINNING AT THE FROG'S ABDOMEN.

COOOOL...

AMEND

117

WHAT'S WITH YOU?

WE HAD TO DISSECT FROGS IN BIOLOGY TODAY.

SO?

SO I WAS A LITTLE DISTURBED BY THE EXPERIENCE, OK?!

BECAUSE IT GROSSED YOU OUT?

BECAUSE I REALLY, REALLY, REALLY **LIKED** IT.

EEW. NOW **I'M** DISTURBED.

THERE WAS JUST SOMETHING ABOUT SEEING THOSE CUTE LITTLE KIDNEYS...

AMEND

MOM, YOU KNOW HOW I HAD TO CUT UP A FROG IN BIOLOGY?

YES...

SUPPOSE I REALLY LIKED DOING IT. I MEAN, **REALLY** LIKED DOING IT. REALLY, REALLY, **REALLY** LIKED DOING IT. WHAT WOULD THAT MEAN?

WELL, MAYBE THAT YOU'D MAKE A GOOD SURGEON.

AMEND

OH. I HADN'T THOUGHT OF THAT.

OR A GOOD AX MURDERER.

AAAA! I KNEW IT!

PAIGE, HE'S **KIDDING.**

DIDN'T JACK THE RIPPER TAKE BIOLOGY?

MOTHER, I ACTUALLY **ENJOYED** DISSECTING A FROG!

SO?

SO?! SO DON'T YOU THINK THAT MAKES ME JUST A LITTLE **WEIRD?!**

ASSUMING YOUR ENJOYMENT WAS MORE INTELLECTUAL THAN VISCERAL, IT PROBABLY JUST MEANS YOU'RE STARTING TO LIKE SCIENCE.

AMEND

AND **THAT** DOESN'T MAKE ME WEIRD?!

AS MUCH AS YOUR BROTHERS MIGHT SEEM TO PROVE OTHERWISE...

LOOK— GRAVITY!

...THEN AFTER WE **REMOVED** THE FROGS' INTESTINES, WE—...

MMM-MM, GREAT SPAGHETTI, HON.

FROG KILLER.

FROG KILLER.

FROG KILLER.

I SEE YOU'RE EXPANDING YOUR REPERTOIRE.

NOT BY MUCH.

MOM, JASON'S CALLING ME A FROG KILLER.

JASON, GET IN HERE!

THE FROG WAS **ALREADY** DEAD. ALL **I** DID WAS DISSECT IT. SO I THOUGHT IT WAS COOL—BIG DEAL!

I MEAN, AT LEAST IT DIED SO I COULD STUDY FROG PHYSIOLOGY. I CAN THINK OF BIGGER WASTES OF LIFE.

SPEAKING OF WHICH...

YOU RANG?

JASON, THIS IS WHAT— OUR THIRD LITTLE CHAT TODAY?...

FoxTrot

by Bill Amend

FoxTrot

by Bill Amend

UM, DAD?

MAYBE YOU SHOULDN'T HAVE GOTTEN SUCH A FAT TREE.

QUIET. PETER, ARE YOU READY?

READY.

OK— PULL!

MMMF!

PULL!

MMMF!

P—...

KKRKRKRFFT!

AS I WAS SAYING...

WHERE DOES YOUR MOTHER KEEP THAT PLANT FOOD?

MAYBE IF WE SAWED OFF THE BOTTOM FIVE FEET..

121

WHAT'S IN THE BAGS?

CHRISTMAS LIGHTS, ANDY.

EVER SINCE I WAS A LITTLE KID I'VE DREAMED OF HAVING ONE OF THOSE HOUSES WITH THE BILLIONS OF LIGHTS AND THE ROBOT SANTAS.

WELL, I'VE GOT THE LIGHTS AND I'VE GOT THE DESIRE. NOW ALL I NEED TO DO IS GET MY BUTT UP ON THAT ICY ROOF.

OF COURSE, YOU PICK THE WEEK WHEN I'M OUT OF TUMS.

WE'VE GOT A 220-VOLT OUTLET, RIGHT?

ROGER, WHAT KIND OF CHRISTMAS LIGHTS ARE THESE?!

AH, YOU ALREADY NOTICE A DIFFERENCE.

PRESENTING THE NOËL-BLASTER SERIES 250XB OUTDOOR HOLIDAY LIGHT STRING. EACH 250-FOOT CABLE FEATURES OVER 500 60-WATT HALOGEN BULBS SEALED IN COLORFUL AND AIRTIGHT PLASTIC HOUSINGS.

Noël-Blaster 250XB

GUARANTEED TO WAKE UP THE NEIGHBORS.

FIRE TRUCKS HAVE A WAY OF DOING THAT, YES.

WHAT DO YOU SUPPOSE THEY MEAN BY "CERTIFIED ELECTRICIAN"?

PETER, I WANT YOU TO GO HELP YOUR FATHER HANG ALL THOSE CHRISTMAS LIGHTS OUTSIDE.

WHAT?!

MOM, IT'S LIKE A ZILLION BELOW OUT THERE! WHY DO I HAVE TO DO IT?! WHY NOT JASON?! WHY NOT PAIGE?! WHY NOT YOU?!

WHY DOES IT HAVE TO BE ME?!

BECAUSE YOU KNOW CPR.

WHY ARE THE LIGHTS DIMMING?

DAD, WHY ARE YOU PLUGGING THEM IN **NOW**?

AH, I SENSE A LEARNING OPPORTUNITY FOR SOMEONE.

YOU SEE, PETER, THE **SMART** DECORATIVE LIGHT HANGER-UPPER WILL CHECK FOR BAD BULBS **BEFORE** STRINGING THEM UP, THUS ELIMINATING DIFFICULT LADDER VISITS LATER ON.

OBSERVE. NOW, AS YOU CAN SEE, THIS ENTIRE STRING IS DEAD. AREN'T YOU GLAD WE CHECKED IT OUT FIRST?

ROGER, THE TV JUST WENT OUT.

ABOUT THIS BEING A LEARNING OPPORTUNITY...

OH, GOOD— IT'S JUST THE FUSE.

DAD, YOU KNOW HOW YOU WERE EXPLAINING TO ME THE TWO COMPETING SCHOOLS OF THOUGHT ON HANGING CHRISTMAS LIGHTS..

HOW IT'S THE "QUICK AND SLOPPY" STYLE VERSUS THE "SLOW AND ELEGANT" STYLE...

ARE YOU SURE THERE'S NOT A **THIRD** STYLE?

PHEW. CAN YOU BELIEVE I'VE BEEN UP HERE FOR SIX HOURS?

BY THE WAY, ARE SANTA'S BOOTS RUBBER?

WELL, IT TOOK ME NINE HOURS OUT ON THE ROOF IN SUB-ZERO WEATHER, BUT THE LIGHTS ARE ALL UP.

YESSIRREE, ALL 3,000 FEET OF OUR NEW NOËL-BLASTER 250XB HALOGEN LIGHT STRINGS ARE UP, SECURED, TIGHTENED AND READY FOR ACTION. IT'S A SPECIAL FEELING.

THIS JUST IN...

THE MANUFACTURER OF THE NOËL-BLASTER SERIES 250XB HALOGEN CHRISTMAS LIGHT STRING HAS ISSUED AN IMMEDIATE RECALL DUE TO SAFETY CONCERNS. SAYS A COMPANY SPOKESMAN: "DO NOT USE THESE LIGHTS. PERIOD."

YET ANOTHER SPECIAL FEELING?

YOU KNOW, THEY STILL LOOK GOOD TURNED OFF...

NOW BACK TO "IT'S A WONDERFUL LIFE"...

by Bill Amend

FoxTrot

OOO—PIERRE! A NECKLACE OF 172 IDENTICAL HAND-STRUNG PEARLS!

END THAT WHAS JAHST EH STAH-KENG STUFFAIR.

OOO—PIERRE! THEY'RE BEAUTIFUL!

AH, OUI. AH SCOWAHRD THE SAYVAHN SASE FAHR THESE PEARELLS.

OOO—PIERRE.

END THESE...

OOO—PIERRE.

END THESE...

OOO—PIERRE.

END THESE...

ZZZZ... OOO—PIERRE... ZZZZ...

AS THEY SAY IN COWBOY MOVIES, "YEEHA."

THE TRICK WILL BE VANISHING INTO THE SUNSET.

AMEND

I DON'T KNOW WHICH IS WORSE.

HMM?

JASON'S 2,792-ITEM CHRISTMAS LIST WITH ITS CROSS-REFERENCING INDEX AND COLOR-CODED CHAPTER TABS...

OR?...

OR PETER'S **ONE**-ITEM LIST.

UH-OH.

OK, I CALLED GUITAR WORLD AND THEY'VE GOT ONE IN STOCK...

PETER, LOOK, ABOUT THIS ELECTRIC GUITAR YOU WANT FOR CHRISTMAS...

NEVER MIND.

COOOOL.

I ALSO HAVE THESE FAKE ZOMBIE **TEETH**...

♪ YOU BETTER WATCH OUT... YOU BETTER NOT CRY...

♪ YOU BETTER NOT POUT... I'M TELLIN' YOU WHY...

♪ SANTA QUINCY'S CO-MINNG TO TOWWN...

AAAA!

SHE'D BETTER WATCH OUT?!?

I WOULD CALL THAT POUNDING BOTH NAUGHTY **AND** NICE.

LOOK, ROGER— CAROLERS!

REALLY?

IT'S BEEN YEARS SINCE THEY'VE COME DOWN OUR STREET.

THEY USED TO COME ALL THE TIME. I WONDER WHY THEY STOPPED.

WRIST ROCKET READY...

READY...

UM, I BLINKED. DID I MISS IT?

'TWAS THE DAY AFTER CHRISTMAS...

AND ALL THROUGH THE HOUSE...

NOT A CREATURE WAS STIRRING...

FOR GOOD REASON, I SUPPOSE.